2

Pam Wedgwood's
RecorderWorld

Very first adventures in recorder playing

by PAM WEDGWOOD

illustrations by DREW HILLIER

www.recorderworld.co.uk

Music notation is given in both
English and American terminology throughout

CD notes: Some shorter pieces are combined on one track
All concert pieces have rehearsal and performance tempo tracks

© 2003 by Faber Music Ltd
First published in 2003 by Faber Music Ltd
3 Queen Square London WC1N 3AU
Cover design by Shireen Nathoo Design
Music processed by MusicSet 2000
Printed in England by Caligraving Ltd
All rights reserved

ISBN 0-571-52239-4

To buy Faber Music publications or to find out about the full range of titles
available please contact your local music retailer or Faber Music sales enquiries:

Faber Music Limited, Burnt Mill, Elizabeth Way, Harlow, CM20 2HX England
Tel: +44 (0)1279 82 89 82   Fax: +44 (0)1279 82 89 83
sales@fabermusic.com   fabermusic.com

This book belongs to

_____

FABER *ff* MUSIC

Welcome back to RecorderWorld!

Are you ready for more exciting adventures in RecorderWorld?

Here are the notes you have already learnt – fill in the note names underneath each one:

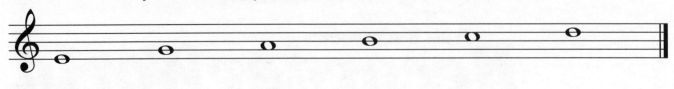

But there is lots more to learn! So grab your recorder, and let's get started…

Summer goodbye
English traditional

Revision rag

RAGTIME …

… is nothing to do with old clothes or dusting! It was a style of music that was popular in America in the early 1900s.

CLAP AND COUNT

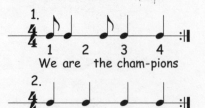

Concert time

FACT FILE

D.C. al Fine ('fee-nay') means go back to the beginning and play to the *Fine* (end).

D.S. 𝄋 means go back to the sign 𝄋.

River boat shuffle

Cheerfully

p

FINE

f

p

D.C. al Fine

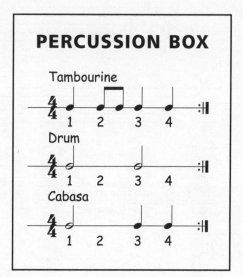

PERCUSSION BOX

Tambourine

4/4   1   2   3   4

Drum

4/4   1   2   3   4

Cabasa

4/4   1   2   3   4

QUICK QUIZ

If you blow too loudly, what happens?

Should you use a 'doo' or 'tut' tongue to play *staccato*?

Should you use a 'doo' or 'tut' tongue to play *legato*?

PLAYING SKILLS

Always remember to sit or stand up straight. This will help to support your breathing.

New note F sharp

FACT FILE

When a **SHARP** ♯ is written in front of a note it is called an **ACCIDENTAL**.

A sharp raises a note by a semitone (half a tone, half step).

F sharp rock

With a strong beat

TOP TIP

An accidental like F sharp applies to ALL the Fs in that bar.

Here's the outline of a piece; see if you can finish it off by yourself.

FINGER CRUNCHER

Practise this lots of times to get your fingers going!

Concert time

FACT FILE

A key signature is the group of sharps or flats (see Stage 5) at the beginning of every stave/staff – it tells you what **KEY** the piece is in.

Notice the key signature at the start of *Tallis' canon*? It is in G major, so every F in this piece becomes F sharp.

Tallis' canon   A round or 'canon' is a piece in which several players have the same music but start one after the other. Group 2 start when group 1 have got to figure 2, and so on.

TOP TIP

Tallis' canon starts with an **UPBEAT/PICK-UP**, or the fourth beat of the bar/measure. Count 1-2-3 then in!

Space walk

PIANO ACCOMPANIMENT

PERCUSSION BOX

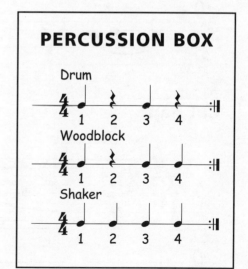

Drum

Woodblock

Shaker

Dotted notes

CLAP AND COUNT

$\frac{3}{4}$

Rock - a - bye

FACT FILE

When a dot is written beside a note, it makes it longer by **HALF** as much again. So:

= 1 beat + half-beat = 1½ beats

Rock-a-bye baby!

Jazz waltz

PIANO ACCOMPANIMENT

p

f

TOP TIP

This piece is in G major. Remember all Fs become F sharp.

Cat nap

Sleepily

p

1.

2. **slowing down**

snore

PERCUSSION BOX

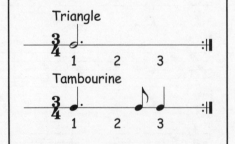

Triangle

$\frac{3}{4}$ 1 2 3

Tambourine

$\frac{3}{4}$ 1 2 3

6

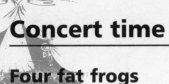

Concert time

Four fat frogs

Happily

Four fat frogs played hap - pi - ly, leap -

frog - ging a - round, not mak - ing a sound. Then four fat frogs fell

fast a - sleep and dreamt_ of hav - ing lots to eat!

Fandango

With a Spanish feel!

Recorder 1

Recorder 2

CLAP AND COUNT

Four fat frog - gies

GROUP WORK

✧ Divide into 2 groups.

✧ Group 1 claps the rhythm of the top line of the Fandango.

✧ Group 2 claps the pulse.

7

New note low D

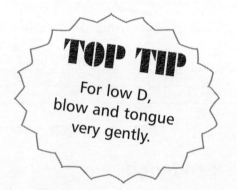

Dynamo rock

With a strong beat

TOP TIP

For low D, blow and tongue very gently.

London's burning

Lon-don's burn-ing, Lon-don's burn-ing, fetch the en-gines, fetch the

en-gines. Fire, fire! Fire, fire! Pour on wa-ter, pour on wa-ter.

Concert time

TRUE OR FALSE?

	✔	✗
F sharp is a tone/whole step higher than F	—	—
This rest is worth half a beat: ⅞	—	—
♩. = 2 beats	—	—

Simple gifts †

American traditional

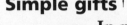

In march time

p

f

Irish melody

Flowing

p

f

p

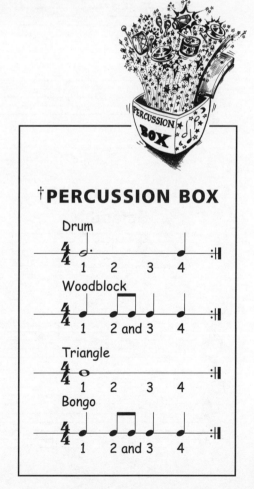

† PERCUSSION BOX

Drum

Woodblock

Triangle

Bongo

9

New note B♭

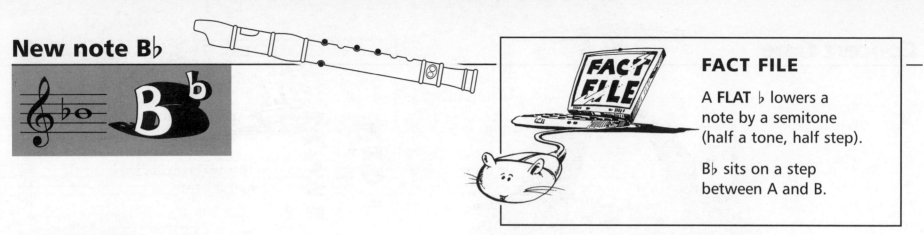

FACT FILE

A **FLAT** ♭ lowers a note by a semitone (half a tone, half step).

B♭ sits on a step between A and B.

B flat boogie

Boogie on down!

FINGER CRUNCHER

Coventry carol

Smoothly

FACT FILE 2

This is a pause/fermata:

It means hold the note for longer than its written value.

10

Concert time

FACT FILE

This is a **NATURAL**: ♮

A flat or sharp is cancelled out by a natural sign.

Make way for the Queen

Quite slow

PIANO
ACCOMPANIMENT

TOP TIP

Remember all Bs in this piece are flat, unless cancelled out.

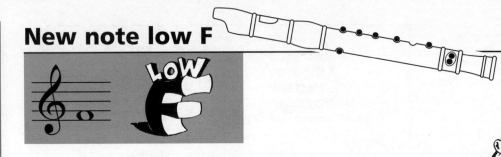

STAGE 6

New note low F

FACT FILE

Watch out for the key signature! These pieces are in F major, so all the Bs are flat.

Sleeping F

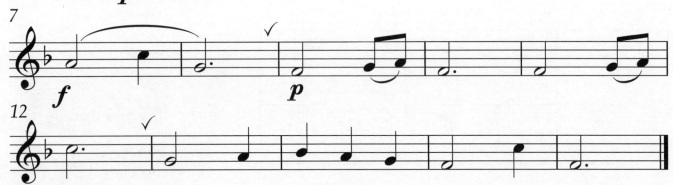

FINGER CRUNCHER

Blow and tongue very gently.

Hip hop

TOP TIP

If your recorder is made in three sections, twist the end joint round until the hole is in the correct place for your little finger.

Concert time

Carnival of Venice

Giulio Briccialdi

Kalinka

Russian traditional

STAGE 7

New note C sharp

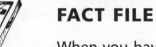

FACT FILE

When you have a C sharp in the key signature, it looks like this:

Twilight zone

FINGER CRUNCHER

Traffic jam

In this piece, choose your own notes.
*A thin line means **p**, a thick line means **f**.*

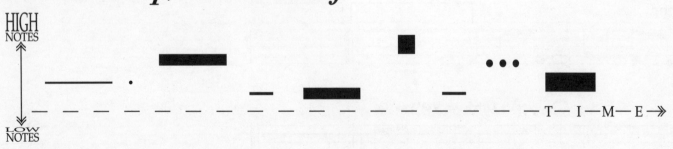

TOP TIP

For C#, make sure your recorder is balanced securely on your right thumb!

14

Concert time

Can can

Jacques Offenbach

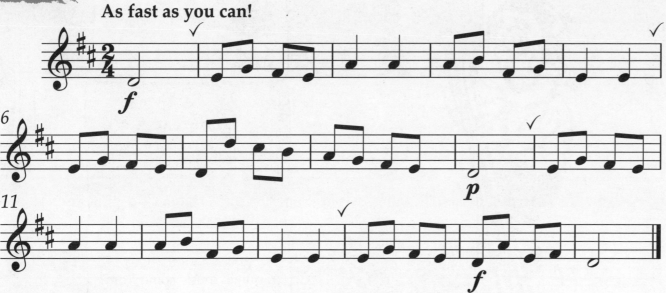

TOP TIP
Watch out for the key signature of two sharps! This means the piece is in D major.

Rhythm bingo

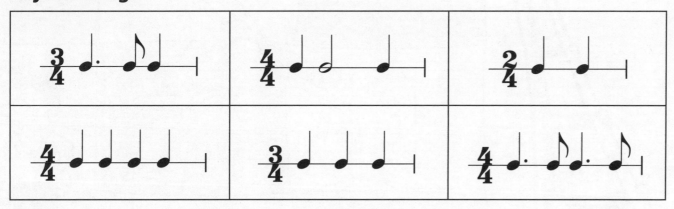

How to play rhythm bingo

Listen to your teacher play each of these rhythms; they will need to give you the pulse first.
When you hear one, cover it up. The first person to have all the rhythms covered shouts BINGO!

Here's what you do:

Roll a die and move around the board, doing the quick quizzes along the way. If you get an answer wrong; go back 2. If you get it right; hurrah, move on 2!

(Watch out for the recorders and ladders that will back-track or fast-track you along the way ...)

What does *D.C. al Fine* mean?

TRUE or **FALSE**
D major has a key signature of 2 sharps

Which country does 'ragtime' music come from?

Draw a quaver/ eighth note rest

How many semitones/half steps are there in a tone/whole step?

Start here

FINISH

TRUE or FALSE
a dot beside a
note makes it
1 beat longer

Go back and play
Four fat frogs

What does
this symbol

mean?

Flats and sharps are called

A_ _ C I D _ _ _ _ _ A_ _ S

What cancels
out a flat or
a sharp sign?

What is an
upbeat/pick-up?

Go back and play
Revision rag

Classical music

FACT FILE

Allegro = quite fast and lively

Vivace = even faster than *Allegro*!
('viv-archay')

William Tell overture

Gioacchino Rossini

Allegro

PIANO
ACCOMPANIMENT

Ode to joy

Ludwig van Beethoven

Vivace

PLAYING SKILLS

From now on,
try putting
in your own
breath marks before
playing each piece.

'Sing' the piece through
in your head first.

Rests

The Saints

Spiritual

With spirit

f

O when the saints, go march-ing in, O when the

f

saints go march-ing in; I want to be___ in that

p

f

num-ber,___ O when the saints go march-ing in!

f

REST REMINDER

▬	= count a silent bar/measure
▬	= count 2 silent beats
𝄽	= count 1 silent beat
𝄾	= count half a silent beat

TOP TIP

To remember the difference between

▬ and ▬

think: if it's hanging, hang on for longer!

New note top E

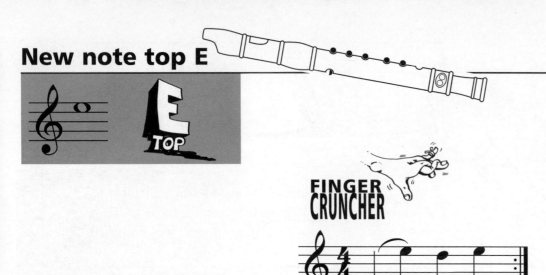

E TOP

PLAYING SKILLS

To play top E, finger low E, then bend your LEFT thumb at the joint and press your thumbnail into the hole, creating a little opening at the top. This is called **HALF-HOLING** or **PINCHING**. It will take some practising!

The distance from low E to top E is eight notes, or an **OCTAVE**.

A pentatonic scale

Try playing this staccato, legato and from memory

Lotus blossom

Peacefully

PIANO ACCOMPANIMENT 84

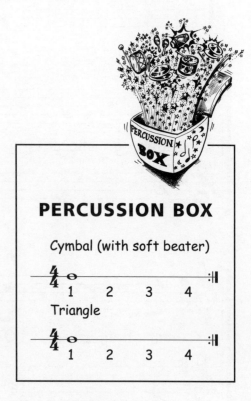

PERCUSSION BOX

Cymbal (with soft beater)

4/4 1 2 3 4

Triangle

4/4 1 2 3 4

In a Japanese garden

Try making up your own piece using the five notes of the pentatonic scale. This is called improvising. Here are some starting points; try playing them in any order, then make up some ideas of your own. Think of an imaginative title for your piece, and perform it to your friends.

PIANO ACCOMPANIMENT 85

FACT FILE

A **SCALE** (originally meaning 'ladder') is a set of notes that go up and down by step.

A pentatonic scale has five different notes (top E and low E count as one). It is used particularly in Eastern music.

New note top F

Bucket and spade blues

FACT FILE

This sign > is called an **ACCENT**. Tongue a little harder to 'attack' the start of the note.

FINGER CRUNCHER

TOP TIP

Remember: For low F, on with the little finger – for top F, don't let that finger linger!

Concert time

Choc ice serenade

Gentle waltz

86 87
PIANO ACCOMPANIMENT

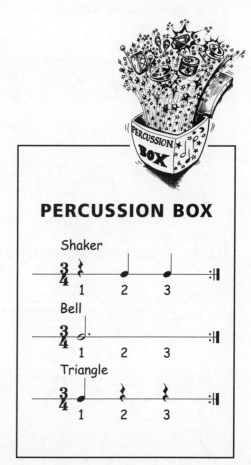

PERCUSSION BOX

Shaker

Bell

Triangle

23

$\frac{6}{8}$ time signature

RHYTHM BANK

Clap these rhythms:

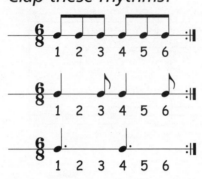

FACT FILE

In $\frac{6}{8}$ there are six ♪ beats, or two ♩. beats in each bar or measure.

When the music is quite slow, count six in each bar/measure.

When the music is quite fast it's a good idea to count in two (one-and-a, two-and-a).

Pop goes the weasel

Lively

Half a pound of tup-pen-ny rice, half a pound of trea - cle: that's the way the mo - ney goes, pop goes the wea - sel!

Row, row, row your boat

Traditional

Row, row, row your boat, gent - ly down the stream.
Mer -ri - ly, mer ri - ly, mer -ri - ly, mer ri - ly, life is but a dream.

Concert time

Six little pigs went to London

QUICK QUIZ

What's the highest note in this piece?

What's the lowest note?

The distance between these notes is called an

O _ T _ V _

Six little pigs stayed at home

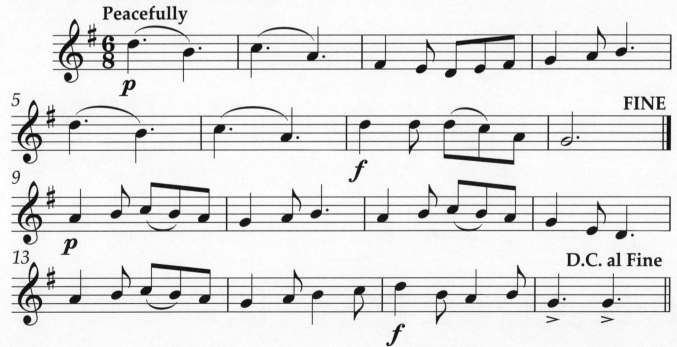

New note low C

FACT FILE

Low C sits on a little line called a **LEDGER LINE**.

Ledger lines are used above or below the stave/staff for notes that are too high or too low to be written on it.

Scale of C major

Try playing this both staccato and legato

Pitch game

Do you know this tune? Can you complete it 'by ear'?

FINGER CRUNCHER

Sweet and low

Gently

PIANO ACCOMPANIMENT [90]

TOP TIP

For low C, blow very GENTLY and QUIETLY, using a 'doo' tongue. If the note sounds squeaky, make sure your fingers are covering all the holes.

Concert time

Now is the month of Maying

Thomas Morley

New note top F sharp

PLAYING SKILLS

To play top F sharp, finger G and add the middle finger of your right hand.
Then **PINCH** the thumbhole.
You will need to blow quite hard!

FINGER CRUNCHER

The sizzling sausages song

PIANO ACCOMPANIMENT [91]

With an appetite!

f   *p*

5

f

Take it easy

PIANO ACCOMPANIMENT [92]

Relaxed

p

1.

7

2.

New note top G

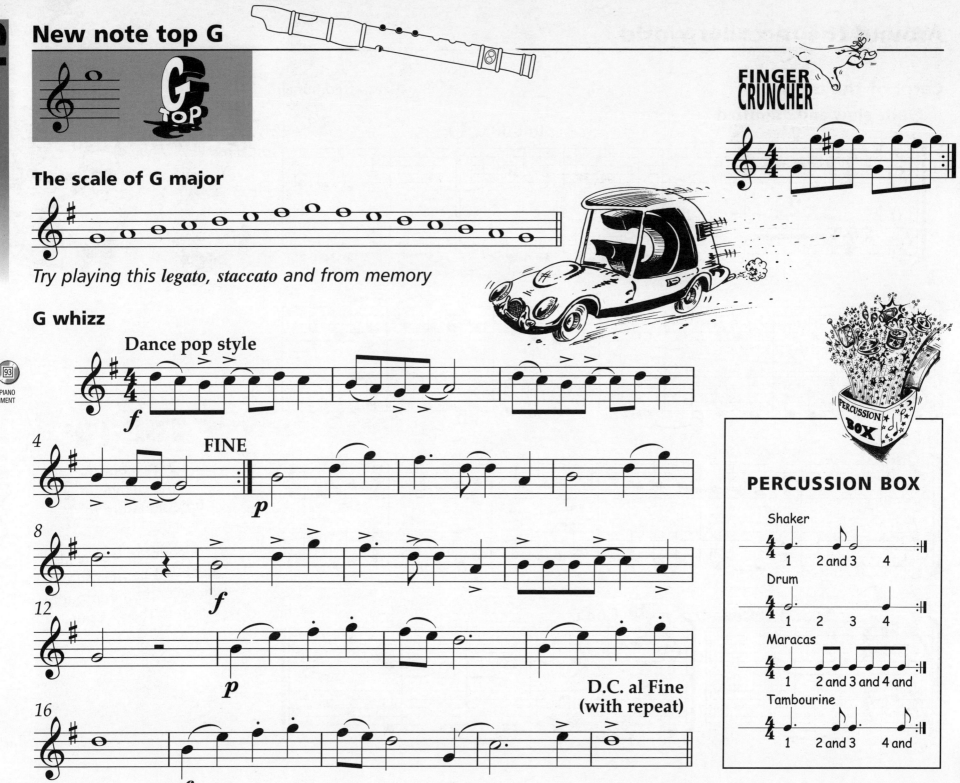

The scale of G major

Try playing this legato, staccato and from memory

G whizz

Dance pop style

FINE

FINE

D.C. al Fine
(with repeat)

FINGER CRUNCHER

PERCUSSION BOX

Shaker
1   2 and 3   4

Drum
1   2   3   4

Maracas
1   2 and 3 and 4 and

Tambourine
1   2 and 3   4 and

Around the recorder world

Carol of the drum

Czech traditional

Quite slow and dignified

TOP TIP

Watch out for the change of time signature to $\frac{2}{4}$:

count in steady ♩ beats. At bar/measure 5 (the second time through), skip to the ⊕ **Coda**.

Karibuni

With a steady beat

PERCUSSION BOX

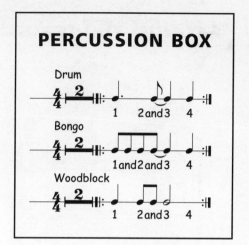

Mango walk

Jamaican traditional

Allegro

Name _____

CONGRATULATIONS!

You've now completed your adventures in **RecorderWorld**.
We hope you've enjoyed yourself along the way.
Visit www.recorderworld.co.uk for a free mystery tune!

From all your friends in **RecorderWorld**.

SIGNED (teacher)

_____

(date) _____